THE UNSAID BETWEEN A PARENT AND A CHILD

ANANYA ANURAG ANAND
SANKALITA ROY

Dedicated to my parents, who have instilled in me the quality of being thought-provoking! They have instilled in me the curiosity of asking questions and the courage to seek answers.

Contents

Preface — *vii*

Acknowledgements — *ix*

Prologue — *xi*

1. Life's Heaven When We Are Together! -Ananya Anurag Anand — 1

2. Unsaid Things To The Toxic Parents -Sankalita Roy — 5

3. Sugar Cubes And Five Rupees -Debomita Sadhu — 9

4. Five Lessons From My Life As A Kid -Arun Kunjunny — 13

5. Seven Golden Rules Of Parenting -Eliam Hartwell — 18

6. The Shocking Epiphany -Anushka Banerjee — 21

7. Small Gestures, Big Impact -Aayudhi G Kanabar — 25

8. A Gift From Her Heart -Anwesha Rath — 27

9. Echoes Of Silence: Bridging The Emotional Gap Between Parents And Children -Omkar Arali — 29

10. Navigating Generational Comments -Juno Ashok — 36

11. The Unspoken Pain Between Parents And Children -Vidushi Yadav — 39

12. Unheard Echoes: A Daughter's Quest For Identity And Acceptance -Varshaa Arer — 43

13. Lost In Words -Subhrajeet Lenka — 49

14. Unspoken Words: The Silent Chasm Between Parent And Child -Neel Deshpande — 51

15. Pillars Of Life: Ma And Pa -Promila Sutharsan — 55

Contents

16. Father's Happiness..! -S. Ramasamy   60

17. The Urge To Live A Teenager's Life -Khushi Sindhi   65

18. Bridges Of Understanding: Tales Of Love And   69

     Reconciliation -Ms. S V Padhmalatha

19. The Silence Of Addiction -Tejaswi Kalra   75

20. Lessons Learned, Lessons Passed -Darshana Hegde   78

Afterword   83

Preface

The idea for "The Unsaid Between a Parent and a Child" has been growing in my mind for many years, fueled by my own experiences and observations. The word "Unsaid" captures the delicate, often indescribable aspects of the parent-child relationship that are rarely spoken about yet deeply felt. Writing this book has been both a challenge and a joy as I sought to articulate the nuances of these relationships and explore the silent understanding that often exists between parents and their children. My hope is that this book will offer readers a deeper appreciation of the bonds that tie us to our families, and perhaps inspire new conversations and reflections.

Acknowledgements

Writing "The Unsaid Between a Parent and a Child" has been a journey of reflection and growth, and I am deeply grateful to everyone who supported me along the way.

First and foremost, I want to express my heartfelt thanks to my parents, whose unwavering love, wisdom, and guidance have shaped my life in countless ways. This book is, in many respects, a tribute to the lessons they've imparted and the bond we share.

I am also indebted to my friends and mentors who encouraged me to pursue this project, offering their insights, feedback, and unwavering belief in my vision. Your support has been invaluable.

Finally, to every parent and child who has inspired this work, your stories and experiences are the foundation upon which this book is built. Thank you for allowing me to explore and share the profound connection that exists between us.

Prologue

The unsaid is a silent thread that weaves through the lives of parents and children. It is in the knowing glance exchanged between a mother and her child, the comforting touch of a father's hand, and the unspoken understanding that binds a family together. I was a child, perhaps no older than six, when I realized that the bond I shared with my parents was not merely one of duty or expectation but something far deeper and more profound. It is this discovery, and the countless others that followed, that inspired me to explore the unsaid and share its meaning with you all.

1

Life's heaven when we are together! -Ananya

Anurag Anand

Ananya is currently a Research Scholar at the Indian Institute of Information Technology (IIIT) Allahabad, specializing in Biomedical Engineering and experimenting with antimicrobial peptides. Ananya has made significant strides in both the scientific and literary worlds. Recently, she was honored with an Honorary Doctorate in Literature for her impactful contributions to society through her writing.

Ananya's passion for literature began in childhood, and she has been an active writer ever since. Her first book, titled *PURPOSE*, was published in 2019, marking the beginning of her journey as an author. Through her work, she has continuously explored the intersection of science, literature, and social change, using her platform to inspire and engage with a wide audience.

Her work has earned her several accolades, including the Best Author Award 2021 by NMCBI for her book *Menstruation: A Consciousness That Is Experienced Unconsciously*, which explores the connection between the menstrual cycle of a woman and spirituality. Recently, she was honored as the Non-fiction Woman Writer of the Year, 2023 by Ukiyoto for her book *What Comes After Marriage?*, a poignant exploration of the stigmas surrounding marriage, particularly for women in India.

Her unique blend of scientific inquiry and literary expression has earned her recognition and respect in both fields, making her a dynamic and influential figure in academia and beyond.

Please visit her blogs at www.sciefiindia.blogspot.com

𐏒𐏒𐏒

Life's Heaven When We Are Together!

The bond between parents and children is one of the most profound connections in life. It's filled with love, care, and mutual dependence. Yet, often, there are unspoken words that lie beneath the surface, creating a chasm of misunderstanding and missed opportunities for deeper connection.

As children, we look up to our parents as our first teachers, our protectors, and our guides in this world. They are the ones who shape our earliest understanding of life and help us navigate its challenges. But as we grow, our thoughts, feelings, and experiences begin to diverge, leading to moments of confusion and frustration. We may struggle to articulate our emotions, fearing that we won't be understood or that our feelings will be dismissed.

For parents, the journey of raising a child is filled with hopes, dreams, and expectations. They want the best for their children, often projecting their desires and ambitions onto them. However, in their earnestness to guide and protect, they might inadvertently overlook the individual needs and struggles of their children. The desire to see their child succeed sometimes blinds them to the silent cries for understanding and acceptance.

One of the most common sources of this unspoken tension is the pressure to conform to certain standards. Parents, wanting their children to succeed, may push them to excel in areas they themselves value. They may not realize that the child is overwhelmed, struggling not just with the academic or social expectations but with the need to please their parents. The child, on the other hand, may internalize these pressures, leading to feelings of inadequacy and frustration. The silent plea for recognition of their unique strengths and weaknesses goes unheard.

Similarly, children often fail to express their appreciation for the sacrifices their parents make. They may take their parents' efforts for granted, assuming that they will always be there, silently bearing the weight of the family's needs. The unsaid words of gratitude and love can create a sense of distance, as parents may feel unappreciated or undervalued.

The key to bridging this gap lies in open communication. It requires both parents and children to step out of their comfort zones and engage in honest conversations. Parents need to listen without judgment, to understand the challenges their children face, and to offer support rather than criticism. Children, in turn, need to express their feelings, to share their fears and aspirations, and to acknowledge the efforts their parents make.

When these unsaid words are brought to the surface, the bond between parent and child can strengthen. There is no greater joy than realizing that despite the differences in thoughts, despite the generational gap, the love between a parent and child is unwavering. It's a love that transcends words, but one that flourishes when nurtured with understanding and respect.

In this shared understanding, life indeed becomes a heaven. The journey of life, with all its challenges and joys, becomes more bearable when traveled together, with mutual respect and open hearts. So, let us strive to break the silence, to speak the words that matter, and to cherish the time we have together. After all, life's heaven when we are together!

2

Unsaid things to the toxic parents - Sankalita Roy

Sankalita Roy is an author, an English language trainer and an animal welfare worker from Kolkata in India. She is on her mission to brainwash people with the beauty of life and sharing her thoughts as it is in an authentic way. Her debut book, *Some Unbothered Truths* has led her to win the award for the title 'Poet of the Year' and her anthology *Kolkata Diaries* has led her to be the 'Best Contributor' in the many volumed series. Her literary contribution has led her to be a part of several anthologies, blogs and magazines. Apart from this, her anthologies have been a part of the eminent book fairs around the world including Kolkata, Delhi and Frankfurt. Please visit her at www.sankalitaroy.com.

ᗐᗐᗐ

Unsaid things to the toxic parents

Mothers are a source of unconditional love and their love can never be replaced by anyone in your life. I have heard this statement repeatedly but they are never felt by me for one reason or another. I lived my entire life in regret for believing the above thoughts.

My mother was just sixteen years old when she separated from my father and I lived within her body then. Her journey of bringing me to the earth till I was in class ten was remarkable. She was a mother who loved and devoted her only child with everything in the world. She filled my life with best education, stylish dresses and luxurious food when she herself lived her life in uncertainty and fear all the time. However, a drastic change took place in her life. She changed for the worst. She started to beat me up for smallest of reasons. I was not allowed to go to school and college properly. Anyhow, I managed to survive the challenges thinking her anger and change to be my own fault. During those times, I didn't have a phone or a television to watch. I only had my pets to look after me. I took a wrong decision of pursuing Science. Little did I know then, that the realization of pursuing Science as a mistake would land me to the day where my mother will reveal her true self. I couldn't forget the words spoken by her and it echoes till date to my ears as I write about them, "What do you feel like you will live your dreams! You have broken my dreams and I will break yours. I will get you married at place where you will be beaten up. You and your child will be on the streets." I was shocked as I could not comprehend to what made her say so or take me for granted for the rest of her life.

Years passed as I gradually worked on becoming the best version of myself. I thought that my mother would change after I won my first award but I was horribly wrong.

My pocket money was stopped. I was accused of stealing when my mother could not find her jewelleries or money. In sickness, no one was there to look after me. I had to beg her to take me to the doctor for the persistent headache which was later diagnosed as tensional migraine. Recently, when my mother overheard my conversation with a student about me teaching her through online mode from home, the Wi-Fi connection was cut off under the excuse that we cannot afford it. I was threatened all along to be beaten up and subjected to constant verbal abuse during my exam's preparation and before appearing for it. I cannot talk to my mother anymore. I dreaded her presence. I cried when she talked nicely to me. I cannot trust her anymore. I am exhausted to the core of my being as I fought this constant battle.

I do not know what the future holds for me but I want to share this message with all the parents out there. Love is never one way; you give and you receive it. The struggles are an integral part of who you are but most importantly, who you become is more important in the process. If you feel that you are struggling so hard to raise a child and that the child will be exactly the way you want them to be, it is a completely wrong notion. If you feel like being a parent gives you the audacity to do whatever you want is completely wrong too. In case of my mother, I never understand her logic but I can never overlook her actions. I cannot trust her ever. To the parents who are struggling hard because they are a single mother or they have faced some kind of abuse due to their lack of financial independence, please work on your healing journey so well that your child never suffers from the unconscious toxicity of yours. Remember, a happy mother will always raise a happy child. Fight your battles, take spiritual or professional help like therapy and so on but please don't be a cause of suffering for your child.

3

Sugar Cubes and Five Rupees -Debomita Sadhu

Debomita Sadhu is a multifaceted woman who is a weaver of poetry, a creature of art, and a software engineer. She can be seen coding during the daytime, but at night, her heart spreads its wings and likes to pen itself. Writing, for her, is way more than a passion; it is an expression at best. Art is her way of sorting out the chaos in her mind. An unusual Murakami follower, she thinks Khaled Hossein is the Charles Dickens of modern literature. She aspires to be admired for the string of words that she weaves poetry with. A rational person with two degrees in computer science, she is convinced that there are literary phrases flowing through her veins instead of blood. She wishes to move even the highest of mountains with her words. A Charlotte Bronte-era feminist who refuses to hate men. She belongs to the city of joy, Kolkata. Roshogolla is her way of making peace during a fight—definitely not by throwing it.

ϼϼϼ

Sugar Cubes and Five Rupees

I wish I was a little girl again. Maybe five, maybe four years old. When you would come back from work, I'd instantly climb into your arms and pat all your pockets to look for a dairy milk chocolate bar. When I'd let you take me to the nearby uncle's little shop to buy me an ice-cream every day, even when the doctor said all my teeth would rot and even though mom would call me "your spoiled little brat". It would never be my intention to make my sweet mother angry, but I did it for the sake of seeing you on my side. You were my rock; I knew for a fact that you would stick around. I liked the fact that you would save me from her every time. I thought this would last for a lifetime. You, being my savior. My messiah. My strong warrior, who'd war with the rotting world, to see the toothless smile on my face.

Yes, you were my best friend. I'd tell you everything, from how I got an A in art and to a D in math. I'd share the world with you. I always thought you'd be my best friend for life. But then five turned into fifteen, and I turned into a rebellious teen.

I often wonder which day it was when you bought me the last chocolate on the way back home from work. When was the last day you picked me and Didibhai up on each arm and gave us a spin? Where are you, Papa? Are you lost? I see you, though. I see you doing important work. I see you reading the newspaper. I see you making important decisions for us.

I often see you coming back from the bank, but I don't find any chocolates for me in your pockets anymore. I see you shuffling through piles and piles of paper, but never through the piles of our photo albums anymore. Were we not meant to be best friends forever? Were we meant to grow apart?

Maybe it started the day I found a red stain on my underwear, and I wondered if I had a difficult disease. This metamorphosis of turning into a woman. I wish I could turn the clock back. Maybe it started the day I was told to keep a secret. A secret for life. A secret from you. The women in my life told me not to tell you this ever, as it was a secret that only women knew about. I tried to argue back. What secret would I not be able to share with my best friend? You were my partner in crime, after all. We would even give your high blood sugar a fight. Don't you remember our deal? A sugar cube in your tea secretly in exchange for a five rupee coin with me?

Our friendship was short-lived, I agree. A few years down the line, and we had already forgotten, I assumed. You, about my sugar cube, and me, about your dairy milk. I took up more classes, and you took up more responsibilities. I made new best friends, and you were left with zero. It was also my blameworthiness, for which I take full accountability now, papa, at the quarter age of twenty-five. I regret not telling you about the girls who bullied me in school. I regret not telling you about the man at the stationery shop who would stare at my chest while talking to me. I regret not talking to you after coming back from school because you were not as cool and trendy as my new friends anymore. The more I drifted away from you, the more faults I would find in you. I hated the fact that you were not a partygoer, the fact that you didn't know about advancing technology, and that you would not let me watch English movies because they had profanities.

Although there are some things that I could never have the courage to tell you, especially about the time I came across the concept of a boyfriend, not because I am afraid of you but because I think you would have mistaken me for a traitor and misunderstood me. Misunderstood the fact that you are replaceable in my life. You are the first man in my life to show me how to strategically cheat at carrom, choose a saree for mom's birthday, and taught me how unconditionally selfless love can be. You are the first man in my life, and quite deservingly so. How could I have told you about a boy who was not even half of a man like you? You are irreplaceable, papa. Must I say it out loud?

Because it is me, now at the highly misunderstood age of twenty-five, that I finally understand why, after a long and hard day at work, you would prefer indulging in poetry. I understand now that poetry runs in my veins. It is through you that I have discovered the magic in words, phrases, alliterations, and similes. I am glad you don't know about advancing technology. Oh, how heartbroken would I have been if I had found you scrolling mindlessly on these palm-sized devices? I am glad to still be learning profanities at the age of twenty-five and being rightfully awed by the creativity possessed in them.

Here I am with a bittersweet taste in my mouth, a hopeful heart, and fearful hands, typing this for you, hoping you would never read this but also hoping you would snatch this letter (let's pretend this was written on handmade paper and not typed on a laptop) and read this in an alternate universe with endless possibilities and pull your little girl in for a hug from her long-lost best friend. Adieu.

4

Five Lessons from My Life as a Kid – Arun Kunjunny

Arun Kunjunny is a Personal Transformation Architect, award winning poet, passionate photographer, soft skills trainer, script writer, aspiring movie director and wanderlust by nature. Eternally curious about everything in this world, he travels the path of words to express his thoughts and emotions. The smallest of instances excite him and he sees something new at each step. He believes that the sheer joy of observation of life around can be one of the key things for a spirited life and concludes it with one of his favorite lines about writing – "I do not write to prove, but to improve"

ᘒᘒᘒ

Five Lessons from My Life as a Kid
It was an eerie silence stuffed with words and sentences. It was not a silence that gave one the creeps, or a silence

laced with sadness. It was an absolute stillness where the words kept bubbling up inside the head but could never make its way into my parents' mind. It was a calmness of anger and frustration at not being heard ever, but yet having to listen to the chaos of irrelevant string of words that I heard being shared with others. I spoke to lifeless objects and living plants, as the doors of my parents' understanding capacity stayed shut.

As a kid, I wished my dad told me what I was getting beaten for. It was no normal whacks but sometimes real severe ones using the branch of the hibiscus tree. Indian parents do feel it as their right to use punishment of any form to make their kids disciplined. A rather stubborn and outspoken kid that I was, I never put my head down or took the aggression that my dad displayed, in silence. It is important for all parents to know that the kid is also learning the ways of the world and with each generation, the exposure levels to life is also changing. I do not expect a parent to tell the kid why he is punished before it is done but it is only fair to let the young soul know why he or she was handed out the thrashing, after. Thrashing need not be physical alone but words can cause more damage too sometime.

Punishments are fine to an extent to bring a youngster in line with certain social norms or to get them to a so-called disciplined state of existence but please explain why it is being done to bring in a level of clarity and also to enable the kid to take ownership of the consequences of his/her actions. Be clear!

"The elder one is very obedient. If he is asked to sit in one place, he will sit until he is asked to move. But, the younger one would pop up in ten different places within seconds if you ask him the same". I always wondered as a kid what this statement implied as my mom shared these same set of sentences to numerous people, mostly in my presence. Was it a testimony to the discipline showed by my elder brother or a rather harsh spotlight on my unruly character? She would always follow it up with a smile or a laugh and the faceless listeners in my memory would join in too. I was the only one who was not amused or happy. Confusion ruled my mind always, as I questioned my character during such interactions. In those moments, I became a subject of mockery and humiliation in front of those callous cheerleaders of individuals who cheered my mom on at this sharing of my restless behavior.

Not everything about a kid needs to be shared with others and definitely not a comparative anecdote featuring two kids in the family. The moment of laughter for others could be the making of an eternal wound in the mind of the kid, who feels embarrassed and humiliated. Be empathetic!

I grew up struggling with health issues. Having had consistent bouts of epileptic seizures till the age of 10, it was tough for me to have a normal childhood. One of the strongest memories I have of that period is that of my mom waking me up somewhere past midnight, and asking me to swallow a big pill which was supposed to bring my fever under control. Sometimes, admissions in hospitals meant 3 or more injections in a day and to the point that my arm had dots from the needle piercing the skin multiple times. Even with all these struggles that I endured as a young boy, it always surprised me to hear my mom telling others about how she struggled because of my health issues. The countless days of sleep she missed as she had to stay awake to monitor my fever and the mental trauma she endured because of my seizure episodes. Even when I accept that all these experiences are real and affected her, I wondered if she deliberately missed out on acknowledging what I went through too. What about all those days of being in a government hospital with rather unhygienic conditions at times, and gulping down tablets and syrups, without questioning it even once. My physical and mental trauma during those days felt ignored and dismissed each time during mom's outpouring of her own struggles.

A parent's struggle handling a kid's health issues are real but please do not lessen the importance of or ignore what the kid is also going through. As a grown up, parents are better equipped any day to deal with the situation but the kid is helpless, confused and frustrated at being confined to a bed. Be supportive!

I have seen my mom celebrating achievements of her friends' kids or even random people with a lot of extravagant expression of emotions. It somehow did not pan out in the same manner when it came to whatever I did in life. Some of those moments like working as the editor of the manuscript magazine of the class during high school days, was robbed off the sheen when she spoke about how she had helped and how even the teacher acknowledged her hand in it. From that time on till now, I have hardly seen her celebrate any of the accolades I have received, with a lot of fervor like she used to do with others. Over the years, it made me feel that whatever I did was not enough and the little kid within me always looked for that validation from my mother more than anyone else.

Whatever a kid achieves, no matter how insignificant it might look to your eyes, celebrate it and let him/her take the limelight. You might have done the major portion of the work in the achievement, but step back to generate the confidence of achievement in that young soul. Be respectful!

Having had a lot of anti-depressants after the long period of epileptic episodes in my life, I had some major battles with my mind as an aftermath. During the numerous occasions I felt like I was losing it, I had gone up to my mom and tried telling her that I was feeling low and feeling like giving up. Her response was always the same no matter how many times I tried sharing the intense and deafeningly loud battles inside my head. "It is all your thoughts and it will go away after a while". She did not want to hear more of what I had to share and went on with her work. I was left to debate within whether I should try to share anymore and it reached a point where I kept my struggles with mental health to myself, as I realized my family was not aware or educated enough in that area and did not care much either because of that.

Mental health is not something that concerns adults only. It is equally relevant to kids too. Whatever a kid shares need not be figments of the imagination always but could be a serious reflection of a war inside the mind. Give time to listen and understand. Sometimes, all that is needed is a supportive and listening parent to the little one struggling to stay stable. Be aware and be attentive!

A traumatic childhood, because the parents are not even aware that their actions and reactions have created an eternal wound in a young soul, is one of the worst things that can happen in life. There is no reset button or time machine, to mend the past. The only thing each parent can do is to learn more about the emotional needs of a kid and keep monitoring passively about his/her mental health. Let us not make the tiny life feel massive burdens of emotional trauma due to lack of awareness and inability for empathetic consideration. A joyful soul is a healthy one, and one which can create wonders in the future!

5

Seven golden rules of parenting -Eliam Hartwell

❦

Eliam Hartwell belongs to Kolkata and is a compassionate researcher. He is a dedicated mentor known for his gentle nature and unwavering honesty. With a heart full of kindness and a spirit rooted in integrity, Eliam approaches his work with a deep sense of responsibility and care. His insights and sensitivity to the world around him are reflected in his writings, where he weaves together the threads of knowledge and empathy. A true advocate for the values he holds dear, Eliam inspires those around him to strive for both academic excellence and personal growth.

♥♥♥

Seven golden rules of parenting

1. Parents could be the best real-life role models for their kids. It is the fact that each parent is being constantly

watched by their kids. They learn many things by carefully watching their parents. As one of the parents, one should know that their body language, tone of voice, and every expression are absorbed by their kids. Now, it is the choice of every parent whether to become enraged or handle the unhealthy situation maturely in front of their child.

2. Discipline is essential in every step of the development of children. It helps the children to learn self-control and develop acceptable behaviors. Establishing some house rules like 'no enjoyment with TV will be allowed until homework' is done' may help the kids to develop their self-control. However, forcing discipline is not a good idea. It is always better to teach children the outcomes of discipline so that they can naturally adopt those habits.

3. Irrespective of whether it is small or big, praising their accomplishments will always make them feel proud. Let the kids know that it is common for everyone to make mistakes and that you still love them, even when you are really disappointed with their behavior. Most parents get engaged in criticizing their kids rather than complimenting them. Parents forget how often they react negatively to their kids on a particular day. One must find ways to praise one's children daily through rewards like passionate hugs, love, and any other compliments.

4. In today's era, most parents get so busy with their professional lives that they hardly get any common family time. Even after office hours, most of them get busy with electronic gadgets. One has to make efforts to make time for their kids. Rather than spending dinner together, everyone enjoys spending quality time alone. It is quite natural for kids not to behave properly if they

aren't getting attention from their parents.

5. As a parent, one has to make their expectations clear to their children. One shouldn't unnecessarily burden their children just to fulfill their own unfulfilled dreams. There is no harm in expressing your feelings, but one has to understand the passion, choice, and capability of their children. Discuss with your children and offer choices. At the same time, each parent needs to be open to their child's suggestions. It is generally found that parents who let their children be involved in the decision-making process are more motivated to make decisions independently. Besides, it is essential to allow kids to do things independently that generally make them feel capable, strong, and confident. One has to let them engage in some simple household work where they find happiness.

6. As a parent, one has to inculcate various traits like honesty, respect, kindness, tolerance and friendliness in their kids. Children should notice how their parents help others without expecting a reward and how to express thanks and compliment others for their support. It is the responsibility of each parent to guide their children and make them realize the difference between the wrong and right things. Parents need to express their guidance because it makes all the difference in how a child receives it and responds back.

7. Like any other relationship, communication is pivotal in the parent-child relationship. As a parent, one shouldn't expect kids to follow everything only because, as a parent, "say so". As much as an adult does, every child deserves clear explanations. One has to find time and patience to explain them; otherwise, kids will wonder about the values of their parents.

6

The Shocking Epiphany
-Anushka Banerjee

Anushka hails from Kolkata and has been passionate about English since school days. She pursued her primary education from Salt Lake School and studied English Honours at Rani Birla Girls' College, Calcutta University. She wishes to meddle into the academic sphere and has the urge to pursue her higher studies in the same field. You can reach out to her at anushkabanerjee892@gmail.com

ᕤᕤᕤ

The Shocking Epiphany

Crimson and magenta hued the ambience of the Chatterjee Residence, the auspicious festival of colors enhanced the joviality of my household members. A pleasant and serene March of 2020 was becoming more and more radiant on that pious day. I, Mr Nikhilesh Chatterjee, a bank clerk by profession, was inhaling with exuberance and delighted in the merry-making between my wife and daughter --- Mrs Trisha Chatterjee and Miss Nishra Chatterjee, the mother-daughter duo respectively.

Essence of camphor and *sandal agarbattis*, mingled the aura as it burnt in front of the household- deity – Lord Krishna.

My 16 year old, Nishra conversed with her mother, "Oh, dear mother! Just have a glance at these colors, they are as bright as you!"

Trisha replied with a smile, "Yes! But these colors will appear brighter if they are smeared on your sweet countenance." Nishra is very much fond of her mother and their mutual compatibility is famous in the entire neighborhood. Music, dance, giggles, eating --- continued and it was an ideal Holi Festival indeed, but actually all the charms were a facade for Trisha. She was secretly suffering from breathing problems from a couple of days; she put a façade of happiness over her face and pretended to be charming just to make Nishra oblivious of her deteriorating health She knew it will make her daughter anxiety-ridden amidst all delight and happiness of the festive season.

The next day when Nishra returned from her piano classes, Trisha finally confided to us about her breathing issues. She was being taken to a physician and was given many tests. **A palm of misery clenched my Chatterjee Residence when it was unfolded that Trisha has been tested COVID positive!** Though the disease was not curable at present, just to bear the patient's pandemic-curing stuff --- the Hospital demanded around 3 crores. Hailing from a middle-class household, it was a financial challenge for us. Things seemed to fall apart!

I gave my best effort to gather a handsome amount of money by engaging myself in the bank's drudgery. It's a bitter truth that everyone has been awarded with a rival, especially in his professional life. Mr. Mukherjee, my colleague always had a cold grievance against me, that I always surely sensed. Circulated rumours had given me a hint that maybe his envy is due to my more public admiration than him. Tactfully the cunning Mr Mukherjee conspired against me and somehow trapped me in the act of forging the bank manager's signature on an important document. Consequently, I was fired from my job without any justice. I was so mentally-broken at that moment due to Trisha's deteriorating health and with the burden to gather 3 Crores within such a short tenure that I did not have the time to prove my innocence. A pathetic incident like this was indeed a challenge for my family, who needed an immense amount of money to quench the thirst of the pandemic that afflicted my wife.

"3 Crores! Nishra, how can we gather such a giant amount of money in such a fleeting time?", I cried and added, "Whatever I had, I've given. Now there's no hope!". After 3 days, the hospital called me up and declared, "Mr Chatterjee, thank you for paying us 3 Crores for the operation." I was bewildered! "Lord, how can the amount be paid? An insolvent poor fellow like me can never pay the amount in such a huge crisis of mine!" I was really baffled and I pondered over the matter. Finally, I got to know the reason. Embraced in anguish and despair --- Nishra confided to me about her act of selling our most exquisite and precious family asset --- the sparkling diamond necklace! She said, "My mother's life is at the zenith of my priority list than any other expensive stuff. Dad, I secretly sold the necklace to gather the sum."

Selflessly Nishra did so but alas! The doctors declared, "Sorry, Mrs Chatterjee is no more!" A storm of thunder and lightning flashed on Nishra's emotional state and gave her a severe jolt. I gave a sarcastic smile and said, "Nishra! You sold the necklace?", she nodded. A **shocking epiphany** awaited for her --- she came to know from me that, Mrs

Trisha Chatterjee is not the biological mother of hers. Actually, Nishra's biological mother, Mrs Anita Chatterjee expired at the time of Nishra's birth and Nikhilesh was forced for a remarriage by his relatives just to prevent the infant Nishra from being deprived of a motherly figure. Consequently and reluctantly, Nikhilesh tied the marital knot with Trisha for the sake of the infant. The shock even accelerated when I revealed to Nishra that the diamond necklace which she sold, was her biological mother's.

I've always wondered that how will I convey this truth to my daughter. I lamented and said, "This is what remains unsaid between a parent and a child!"

<u>MORAL OF THE STORY</u> : The above passage unfolds the fact --- how an unsaid truth between a parent and a child can break the societal stereotype that love flourishes only in blood-ties. The affection between Trisha and Nishra was indeed mutual.

7

Small Gestures, Big Impact -Aayudhi G Kanabar

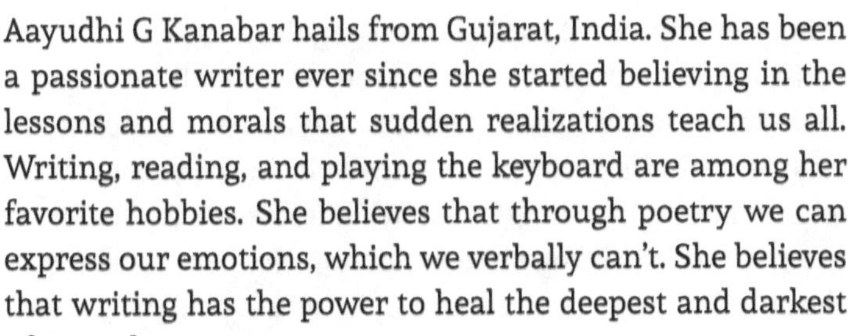

Aayudhi G Kanabar hails from Gujarat, India. She has been a passionate writer ever since she started believing in the lessons and morals that sudden realizations teach us all. Writing, reading, and playing the keyboard are among her favorite hobbies. She believes that through poetry we can express our emotions, which we verbally can't. She believes that writing has the power to heal the deepest and darkest of wounds.

Small Gestures, Big Impact

It is rightly said that parents are the only selfless beings who can see their kids achieving great heights of success. There is no jealousy and no rivalry. But there are many situations where due to minute misunderstandings and perceived generation gap; which are somewhere real;

clashes occur with the modern day's needs and demands. The first major issue is that parents neglect the importance of small victories and the vitality of appreciating small enduring changes. Parents always seek for a change; but they forget to realize that no change is sudden. Many times it is just a gesture saying, 'I am happy that you tried' or 'I am very glad that you did not give up'. These small gestures can surely do wonders. The second most important thing which can resolve many issues between a parent and a child is that parents should at least try to understand the child's point of view. Many times parents are rigid while making many decisions for the child, but just giving an ear to the child and trying to listen to what they have to say can really build self esteem of the child. Most of the time parents even forget to express their love towards the child. There is no doubt that parents always work for the betterment of the child and love them more than anything else in the world but it is even important to show it at regular intervals. On the contrary, sometimes even children are unable to express their love towards their parents, maybe because they are unable to find a medium to express it. In the recent times where there is high inflation it becomes necessary that both the parents work together for giving the best facilities to the child. This is surely essential but due to this the parents are unable to spend quality time with their children and slowly and gradually children start to find their peace and solace in other people and many a times in other things and activities. So to avoid this, parents must take out some time from their day for their children. They should have such a bond that whenever the child makes a mistake he or she should not be afraid of parents but instead should think of confiding it with parents without giving a second thought.

8

A Gift from Her Heart
-Anwesha Rath

A girl from small town but with big dreams dreams is now passionately working in anthologies. Anwesha is just 20 years old and pursuing her graduation. Her only aim is to take care of her parents just like they take care of her. She not just writes poems but also shares heartful messages to people around her. Here she has written a special poem in Hindi language. I'm sure you all will love this masterpiece.

ღღღ

A Gift from Her Heart
Nine months she carried me, a treasure so dear,
In life's great gamble, she faced every fear.
While society may deem her as lost in the fray,
She gave me her all, brightening my way.
What can I ask from the one who's so bold?
Each moment she sacrificed, a story untold.
They label her beaten, but they cannot see,
This lioness rises, so proud and so free.

She drank but water, yet I had the cream,
In a world full of chaos, she followed her dream.
Oh Lord, spare her the depths where sorrow resides,
For the tears that they shed, no love ever hides.
Two years of joy for her nine months of pain,
What do they know of love's sweet refrain?
Those who disregard the mother's embrace,
Can't grasp the beauty of her tender grace.
They boast and they brag, but in truth they don't know,
Before her, my God would humbly bow low.
Shame on those hearts, devoid of respect,
Who tarnish their mother, her love they reject.
No place in the void for such souls who betray,
Those who scorn her honor will surely dismay.
Standing tall they won't, without love in their vein,
For a son who forgets his mother's sweet pain.
What gives them the strength to carry on life?
God turns a blind eye to such a cruel strife.
He hears not the cries of those cruelly unkind,
Who repay love's gift with a heart that's blind.

9
Echoes of Silence: Bridging the Emotional Gap Between Parents and Children –Omkar Arali

Omkar Arali is indeed a storyteller, a dreamer, and a custodian of memories. His words bridge the gap between reality and imagination, inviting readers to embark on their own journeys. At the age of 21, he is conveying incredible stories that connect with the audience.

Starting his writing career with his web series *Devil* during the COVID-19 lockdown, he understood the importance and magic of words. And this magic helped him build his career. For the corporate world, he is a copywriter or content writer; for the storytellers, he is a scriptwriter; for publication houses, he is an author; but for him, he is just a person who writes down his feelings, thoughts, and stories on paper.

With *Our Pets and Us* he started contributing to anthologies, and here is another contribution of his to this anthology, *The Unsaid between a Parent and a Child.*

ᔭᔭᔭ

Echoes of Silence: Bridging the Emotional Gap Between Parents and Children

Most people think saying "I love you" to your parents is one of the hardest things to do. Being an Indian I can confirm this but I just want to add that it's not the most difficult thing.

Because the hardest things to tell your parents are actually the simplest!

Well, hey everyone. I am Omkar Arali, a passionate & versatile writer (copywriter & content writer for businesses, scriptwriter for YouTubers & storytellers, and an author for publication houses). I always believe in the power of words because they can easily create deep wounds in your heart and heal those wounds peacefully. In a world where everyone's trying to influence others with different things, I chose words because that's what I have with me. As a writer, I am passionate about writing stories, and poems that can show a great path for someone to live. Well, today's topic is unique, that is, *The unsaid between a parent and a child.* Hats off to the person who decided on this topic, and now, let's talk about it.

THE TYPICAL INDIAN MINDSET

I am from India, and you know Indian parents are very difficult to understand. You can't predict what they can do and how. They'll love their child a lot but still, they'll choose to beat them or abuse them just because of their silly mistakes.

Indian parents have a shitty concept in their mind that if they'll punish their kids for their mistakes then kids will not repeat it. And at some point, I believe it's okay, but parents should know:

What's the limit of punishment?

What is the topic?

Why has your kid done something that hurts you?

Did he/she do it intentionally?

Did someone force them to do it?

And without knowing all this, parents will still beat their kids. And of course, after some hours they'll tell their kids that they love them a lot and the punishment was necessary. And that's your biggest mistake. See you don't see the scar that's been created in your kid's mind. Now they are afraid of you and THEY WILL NOT TELL YOU ANY SERIOUS THING that you should really know. The mindset is created: If I tell my mom/dad about this, they will beat me. They will abuse me and most importantly, they will not understand me. And here you're failed as a parent and this mindset will always be there in your kid's mind, so be ready to face the worst things that can come to you.

WHY UNDERTSANDING MATTERS?

1 in 5 girls and 1 in 20 boys is a victim of child sexual abuse. Ministry of Women and Child Welfare, supported by the United Nations Children's Fund, Save the Children and Prayas conducted a study to understand the magnitude of child abuse in India, they found that 53.22% of children faced one or more forms of sexual abuse; among them, the number of boys abused was 52.94%.

The most heart-wrenching thing:

Only between 16% and 25% of children disclose the abuse to family and friends during childhood with almost half 44.8% of individuals never disclosing the abuse to anyone

Now you understand the importance of understanding your kid? And if you're thinking it's just about little kids then no, every adult can't disclose such things to their loved ones including parents. And the biggest reasons why kids don't disclose their sexual assault to their parents are guilt, shame, embarrassment & fear! This is the unsaid thing between a parent and a child!

So what can you do?

Just be by the side of your kid, don't punish them in a way that'll leave them with a lifelong scar. Be their friend, be their companion, be their strength, let them know you're always there for them. Build great communication between you and your kid.

WHY ADULTS CAN'T UNDERSTAND THEIR AGED PARENTS?

In my opinion... it's because of lack of COMMUNICATION!

Your kid, even if he's young or just a child, will not agree with some decisions you'll make for him. Because there is a generational gap that you need to understand. What your kid should eat, what he should wear, what he should see and what he should say, these are basic things that you try to control and of course, you should, because *sanskar* or manners matter. But it becomes a problem when you control these things at your kid's young age, When he's exploring the world, making new friends, standing on his own feet, at this time if you control your child, definitely, they'll try to go away from you because it's their life and they want to enjoy it.

Don't think that I am selfish and writing all this for adults but see, I know your kid may not know what's good for him or which type of friends can destroy him but there's a way to tell him. You can't shout at him like a typical Indian dad to stop doing some things and follow your orders, because this will make your kids think that you don't understand them. It will create a mental trauma, an unresolved issue that'll evoke toxicity for you in his mind. And then when you're older, you can't say "My son doesn't understand me. I gave him birth, I gave him food & education and now he's leaving me!"

See, little things matter. Every time you behave with your child will create a memory in their mind that they'll follow in the future. If you tell them not to eat candies, they may eat them behind you. But if you tell them to eat it in specific amounts or tell them why it is bad for them, they'll remember it the next time and will say "Candy is not healthy for me, my mumma said"

So, a parent's each and every action or reaction to their children builds a foundation for their future.

So what can you do?

As I've said earlier, don't try to control them but have a sincere discussion with them. Make sure that the communication between you and your kid is very strong. Let them do things that they love. And if something is bad for them, have a conversation with them. Be calm, and make all eforts to understand them.

Put yourself in your kid's shoes! And this is very important for Indian parents because they may have a bossy attitude towards their children. Be their friend, and then see the change in your relationship.

But there are still many things that can impact the relationship between your child & you such as:

As parents age, their expectations of how their children should behave may differ from the children's own views.

These differences can lead to misunderstandings and strained relationships.

Generational gaps often result in varying values and beliefs. What parents consider essential might not align with their children's priorities, leading to communication breakdowns.

Busy lives, work commitments, and personal responsibilities can cause grown children to unintentionally neglect their parents. The lack of regular communication can create emotional distance.

Mental health challenges, such as depression or anxiety, can affect communication patterns. Both parents and children may struggle to express their feelings effectively.

Sometimes, a significant family event or unresolved conflict can strain relationships. Past hurts or unresolved issues may prevent open communication.

So, according to me, there isn't a specific thing that remains unsaid between a parent and a child, but there are many. To know all those things, strong communication is important. Not a conversation for just a few days but more. It's not something that can be done in a few days or months but it's a lifelong process.

Daily, or at least 3-4 times a week, sit with your kids and talk to him, patiently. Ask them what they're going through. Support them. I know it's not easy but it is important. There can be many things that you'll not like or be able to support but find a good solution that's better for you both.

Don't think about the world or society; think about your kid. He can be innocent, pure-hearted, and may not understand this world but you do. Don't kill his/her innocence with punishments or mental traumas, but make life heaven for the child. You can also tell them about what you're going through or what your issues are. But just make sure that there remains nothing unsaid between a parent and a child.

IN THE END

Whatever is written are my own thoughts and opinions. I don't want to hurt someone's feelings or emotions and if your feelings are hurt by this content, I am extremely sorry. I didn't mean to. In the end, I would like to thank my mom (Shubhangi Arali) and dad (Appasaheb Arali) for making me what I am today. Your love, care & teachings made me able to write this. And to the audience, I wanna say:

Value your loved ones. The one who doesn't have a kid can understand the importance of having one. Don't throw or separate your kid because of your ego, selfishness or society. People are crying, visiting temples, and investing thousands of dollars to get one kid. And if you have one, then value the blessing.

Same for kids, guys. There is no one in this world who can care for & love you like your parents, so value them. Try to understand them. Let them know how much you love them. An orphan can understand the importance of having parents. Ask someone who has lost his/her parents, what it means to have them with you. So if you have your parents by your side, know that you have the most valuable thing in this world with you.

10

Navigating Generational Comments – Juno Ashok

Juno Ashok is a writer hailing from Tamil Nadu, India. She is a writer who never fails to make the readers visualize every moment and every illusion that she conveys.

Being a co-author of more than 50 anthologies, she holds authorship for books like *Rhythms of a Charmaine*, *The Diary of the Predialected didactics*, *Destiny*, *The Shrouded Mirage*, *and The Chimes of Euphoria*. Her books of poetry and stories inspire ideas in the form of social issues, nature, and fantasical amazements.

Her articles have been published in various renounced magazines like Kloud9, Elysian, Ukiyoto, and so on. She has been bestowed with the Best Poet Award by Fanatixx Spectrum, the Best Young Author of the Year Award by Ukiyoto Publications, the Canada Excellence Award by Applause, and many more laurels.

One may reach out to her at @charmaine_of_words via Instagram to enjoy more of her work.

♡♡♡

Navigating Generational Comments

Every child experiences the world through their parents, entering it guided by their presence. Over time, children come to view their parents as their world, and vice versa. However, this beautiful yet delicate connection often becomes entangled. Why does this connection plunge into anger, distance, and silence?

In the era of flourishing generational changes, a significant divide emerges—Technology. With one generation adapting more swiftly than the other, complications arise. Parents, still in the nascent stage of adaptation, resist allowing their little ones to delve deeper. Meanwhile, curious children, eager to explore, grow agitated by the imposed restrictions. This marks the initial instance of distancing.

A prominent, common barrier follows—Comparison. In the competitive world, a healthy environment is demanded, but parents misconstrue it as a challenge. It becomes a source of pride for parents, conquered by their children on their behalf. Little do they realize that each child is unique in their own way.

Societal norms play a pivotal role in influencing the minds of both parents and their children. The clash between carefree attitudes and extreme perspectives becomes a tug-of-war. Neither the younger generation nor the parental mentality is willing to align, hindering potentially alluring changes.

The arrogance in younger ones' behavior stems from numerous direct and indirect factors. Influences from movies, the misinterpretation of heroism, celebrities as role models, and the glorification of villains contribute. Additionally, the inability to distinguish between fantasy and reality, the popularization of unacceptable habits by peers, and the allure of a lavish life all fuel their frustration expressed at home.

Numerous negatives and hurdles exist on both sides of this changing dynamic. Yet, nothing can diminish the purity of parental love, which prevails especially during times when their children undergo physical and mental challenges. Despite parents' attempts to understand and support, they may fall short. It becomes the duty of children to joyfully accept, appreciate, and be grateful for the sacrifices made by their parents to see them prosper.

"Change lies in the hands of both sides."

11

The Unspoken Pain Between Parents and Children -Vidushi Yadav

Vidushi is a storyteller from Varanasi, praised for her compelling stories. Remarkably, this anthology marks the first time she has put her thoughts into writing to share with a wider audience. Vidushi sees this opportunity as the perfect starting point for her writing journey. A firm believer in hard work and Karma, she brings a fresh perspective and passion to her storytelling.

❥❥❥

Unspoken feelings are a common part of family life, yet many parents and children overlook their importance. Emotions like hidden gratitude, suppressed anger, and unexpressed regrets can deeply affect relationships. When feelings are bottled up, they create distance and misunderstandings, making it harder to connect over time. This shows that open communication is essential for healthy family dynamics.

Gratitude is a strong emotion that ties families together, recognizing the love and support shared among them. However, not expressing appreciation can lead to negative outcomes. For example, a child may feel thankful for their parents' support but struggle to express it, thinking their parents already know or feeling awkward about sharing those feelings.

Parents often invest so much of themselves in their children that they may neglect their own needs for recognition. When they feel unappreciated, they may withdraw emotionally, which can confuse their children. The child senses a change but doesn't understand why their parent seems distant.

A simple "thank you" could strengthen the bond between parents and children. Without this expression of gratitude, resentment can grow. Children may feel lost when their parents are emotionally distant, while parents might feel unrecognized for their efforts, leading to a cycle of misunderstandings.

Another common issue is repressed anger. As children grow, they may feel resentful toward their parents for setting strict rules or not providing enough support. Many children find it difficult to express this anger, believing it would be disrespectful. Instead, they bottle up their feelings, leading to emotional rifts.

Parents may misinterpret their child's behavior, thinking their rules are clear and loving. As children act out or withdraw, parents may feel hurt and confused, unsure of what they did wrong. This unaddressed anger can create lasting problems in the relationship.

Improving communication can help bridge these gaps. Parents can encourage discussions about feelings and clarify their intentions. If parents recognize that their children have unspoken grievances, they can invite them to share, making it easier to resolve conflicts. However, when anger remains suppressed, it hinders understanding and healing.

Apologizing is a crucial part of any relationship, especially between parents and children. Acknowledging mistakes and seeking forgiveness can help mend rifts. Yet, some parents hesitate to apologize, fearing it might undermine their authority. This refusal can leave children feeling invalidated and lead to bitterness.

Even when parents realize their mistakes, it can be hard to say sorry. Avoiding apologies only widens the gap and can harm trust. By refusing to acknowledge their mistakes, parents miss the chance to model accountability for their children.

Silent apologies can exist, but they often create distance, leaving both sides feeling disconnected. Over time, this gap can grow, making it harder for children to engage with their parents. Unspoken words can damage relationships that were once built on love.

A sincere apology, even if delayed, can help heal wounds and rebuild trust. Acknowledging a child's feelings opens the door to better communication. It shows parents are willing to grow and learn from their mistakes.

Sharing feelings and regrets is vital to prevent emotional distance. As children grow and responsibilities increase, parents may look back and wish they had spent more time with their kids. While feelings of regret are common, parents often hesitate to share these thoughts, fearing shame or helplessness.

The emotional scars of feeling abandoned can last into adulthood, leaving children questioning their parents' love. They may struggle with feelings of inadequacy and wonder whether they were ever truly appreciated.

12

Unheard Echoes: A Daughter's Quest for Identity and Acceptance -Varshaa Arer

Varshaa invites her readers to embark on a journey of introspection and empathy. Each verse reflects her belief that true wealth lies not in material possessions but in the richness of our values and the depth of our connections. Through her poems, she hopes to inspire us to embrace humility and cherish the simple yet profound moments that life offers.

♭♭♭

Unheard Echoes: A Daughter's Quest for Identity and Acceptance

What hope do I have of convincing you that the way I feel and think is right? Why can't I break that silence? Is it your pride telling you that the young ones can't be right, or do you really want me to suffer through what you have as a matter of legacy? I disagree that women should strive for perfection at all times; in fact, I don't even want to be flawless. Instead, I'd like to assure you that I'm wonderfully flawed in every way that matters to me. Why do you fear I could make an awful decision? Why is it that women like me can't ever have our thoughts taken seriously? **Why do you always assume I'm dumb when I share my thoughts and feelings? Am I just being overly sensitive in the modern world of "hooking up"?** Every woman like me learns to accept praise with poise since their childhood but as I get older, I am exhausted by the tedious task of seeking praises from you. Yes, I do believe that everything about your generation was different! The difference lies everywhere, be it the kitchen or the workplace or the circle of having male buddies to the way that young women have vacations. When I don't do things that you could, why is it a negative thing? Exactly why it is that only females are taught rigid gender norms. Why don't you set me free from all these thoughts? Why don't you see what I'm going through when you tell me I'm wrong? Yes, I do want your time. No! Not for the long boring lectures, but to understand me, to love the things I have, and to clear my thoughts so I can focus.

Please don't expect me to hold the same standards as those who have achieved success before me; I'm just going about things at my own speed. If my results today aren't what you'd expect, they will be in the future. I, too, would like a comfortable income and a place of my own, as well as complete control over my life. I understand that you mean well and want the best for me, but there's no need to be so critical of me every time we have a conversation; why do you constantly compare me to other kids when I don't compare you with their parents? Why do you think, in every case, it's only the parents who make sacrifices for their kids? ...Sometimes it's the kids, too! I realize that my efforts pale in comparison to yours, but I hope you can see that even the smallest of my sacrifices add up to something significant. I have witnessed you both work hard to provide me with the great education and provide the finest possible things that I ask for, fighting against all odds despite the difficulty of the situation. I will never be able to repay your generosity, but I hope to make you both proud of me someday. I want you to know that I am making progress towards my goal, but that the path is winding and challenging, so please bear with me, because that's where you don't understand it. Understand that each individual will be successful at their own pace and in their own way, just as each flower blossoms at its own time.

Please don't rush me; I believe that the best things in life take time, and that everything happens exactly when it's supposed to. Have you ever realised how challenging it would be for me, who is trying so hard to strike out on her own, to make a marriage decision? I'm quite averse to getting married. I want to be self-sufficient; I want to maintain my strength; I want a man who can deal with me as I am. Things won't go the way it did for your generation. Every new generation brings new challenges and opportunities. Adaptation is a "must" for new generations to emerge and that's why our answers would be different. I'm sorry, but I don't want to be on same footing with males; I recognize that men and women are fundamentally wired differently. What I really want is, for him to love me without boundaries, the way you do. I want him to let me spread my wings and soar, and have him share in my joy in my accomplishments, and not a man with male pride who fails to admit that I have done better. Like you taught us not to feel envy or anger towards others, in the same way everyone needs to experience this feeling in order to survive. Certainly, there are some things that can only be done by a woman, but what about the other things you claim girls must endure? Expecting the love I provide is not quaint; it's essential. If he truly cares for me, he will attempt to do these things for me, even if it hurts. This only happens when a man understands the anguish of doing things alone. Please don't come to me with your gender norms and shame me for my expectations from marriage.

I can't stand it when you bring up the subject of you wanting a son "But why?" All Indian parents with daughters must have said this at some point in their lives. Daughters always want the best and wish good for their parents. **Why can't they see that this isn't about gender, but rather about recognizing the value of one's feelings and wishes.** Why do you want a son? Is it for safeguarding you when you're old, or is it because he will carry out your final rites when you die? I don't know who came up with these standards, but every woman must have cursed whomever came up with them. For that reason, I suppose I have tried my hand at some of the things you imagine a son can do for you. But what do I get in the end? All you say is, "I wish I had a son," and that really hurts. I've always aimed to defy stereotypes, not in a negative sense but a positive way, to prove that women are superior to men in every way. Please realise how it impacts my mental health and how it makes me feel like I'm not good enough. Sometimes you make me feel like I can't succeed in anything, and you portray me in a negative light, but why despite all the good things I've done? I realize that neither being famous nor receiving a noble award is in the cards for me, but I still have the urge to attempt new things. If I fail, it will be a learning experience; please don't criticize me for my setbacks.

I'm a girl with ambitions and desire to do something in this life, and I'm not the one to give up lightly on my goals. What more do you want from me? Why do you doubt my superiority when I try to be much better than what I was.

I'm still working out the kinks in my own life, but I know how much it hurts me to see you both turning old. I have thousands of emotions, and I can't find the words to express them. I don't know why you can't see how much your inability to comprehend me bothers me. The more I try to explain things, the less emotional I feel, and if this keeps up, I worry that I'll eventually become heartless. I hope that your inability to see that in me doesn't spell tragedy for me.

It is the parents who decide to start a family, it is your duty to shield your child from such experiences whenever possible. I'm not trying to make excuses for you by stating that you're terrible or failing to give me what I need, but the truth is, you're one of the greatest individuals I've ever met. But please don't misunderstand my silence as a sign of contentment. I am battling inside, so please don't take me for granted even if I seem calm. A note to all parents although I know you only want the best for your children, please remember that you are their home and must always put them first, besides you, who else will take care of this? Now that your kids are older, you shouldn't chastise them like you did when they were younger but rather spend a quality time with them, give an appropriate explanation of right things and reassuring them that they are your first priority. Sure, but don't make them presume again that your presumptions are always correct. Don't use your children's feelings as pawns to prove your views, requirements, or possessions. Get a feel for their motivations and desires as well. You may think this is all foolish because your generation didn't have these things, but keep in mind that even if they suffer through hell without speaking a word, they are still sensitive to the little things that you do, because they value you so highly; there is no one else like you in their eyes. If you can read between the lines and uncover the underlying emotions in their words, you will be the one to bring out the best in them. Saying things like "consider me your friend" all the time isn't realistic, but if you can adjust to the way the world is changing, you'll learn to read your children's feelings in no time.

13

Lost in Words
-Subhrajeet Lenka

❤

Subhrajeet Lenka is a Masters student in Ecology and Environment Studies at the School of Ecology and Environment Studies at Nalanda International University under the Ministry of External Affairs (India), situated in Rajgir, Nalanda District, Bihar. He has a passion for photography, poetry, traveling, and listening to music when not busy with studies. He is a naturalist who likes to live in the lap of nature and loves to compose poetry and prose about the ecological and social aspects of nature and life. He is the author of the book *Harmony of the Words* and co-author of various other books like *Echoes of the Unheard, Memories of Food, Story Spinners Voyage: Words Unleashed, Authors Limelight,* and so much more.

❤❤❤

Lost in Words
Like gloomy skies, no words convey
The pain that deep inside does stay

We sit at the table, eyes that stare
Yet cannot speak the burdens we bear
We long to break free, leave behind
The stigma in the neighbor's mind
Don't mold us to the kid next door
With trauma that we can't ignore
We need just love, a gentle touch
Not races where we're pushed too much
Please understand the lies we tell
To guard the truths we know too well
No dinner fights with anger's flame
Lit by others, shifting the blame
Please hold our hands, don't let us go
Into the sea of sorrow's flow
Understand before you crush
The dreams that in our hearts we hush
We can't face the shattered glass
That pierces as the moments pass
Crying alone, with none to find
A way to soothe the troubled mind
Can't speak of chains that keep us down
Or reach your heart that wears a frown
We only want the colors bright
To fill our lives, remove the night
Without the fights, or hidden things
That silence brings with broken wings.

14

Unspoken Words: The Silent Chasm Between Parent and Child -Neel Deshpande

Who is "Neel Deshpande"?

Is he a Content Creator/ Blogger/ Film Critic or more?

Well, he is hardcore Film Critic.

He says,

"What motivates me? It's *Neel Writes*!

Hello everyone,

I am a person who delivers content writing, content marketing, digital marketing for your brand to scale up high in market.

I have always had a strong, intrinsic urge to put pen to paper. I began publishing my writing online with the hope that it would help other budding writers develop their voices. Today, in addition to being an outlet for my own work, *NEEL WRITES* includes reviews, interviews and more. My specialties include content writing, digital media, public relations, local promotion, and design. My hobbies include writing, watching content, and photography.

These are some of the glimpses of my work:

Film Reviews:

1. https://www.neeldeshpande.in/post/spooky-adventure-with-bhool-bhulaiyaa-2

2. https://www.neeldeshpande.in/post/jalsa-a-women-story

3. https://www.neeldeshpande.in/post/chandramukhi-a-political-love-story

Book Reviews:

1. https://www.neeldeshpande.in/post/book-review-96-metromall-pranav-sakhdeo

2. https://www.neeldeshpande.in/post/prodigal-love-preeti-narang-gets-the-click-of-a-love-story

Covering life journeys:

1. https://www.neeldeshpande.in/post/interview-with-mr-fitness-sagar-gatade

2. https://www.neeldeshpande.in/post/kshitij-patwardhan-a-versatile-writer

3. https://www.neeldeshpande.in/post/fitness-freak-powerlifter-mrs-asha-gupta"

Do reach out to him at www.neeldeshpande.in

ᗐᗐᗐ

Unspoken Words: The Silent Chasm Between Parent and Child

Communication forms the foundation of any relationship, but there exists a peculiar realm of unspoken words that resides between a parent and a child. Despite the close bond they share, this unspoken language carries significant weight, often overshadowing the spoken dialogue. In this essay, we will explore the depths of this intricate phenomenon and shed light on what remains unsaid between a parent and a child.

Related points which need focus:

1. The Burden of Expectations:

Parents, driven by love and concern, often hold high expectations for their children. However, these expectations can create unspoken pressure, instilling fear of disappointment within the child. Parents may hesitate to voice their expectations directly, while children feel the weight of these unspoken desires, straining the relationship.

2. Fear and Vulnerability:

Parents, with the noble intention of protecting their children, often shield them from the harsh realities of life. Unspoken fears, worries, and vulnerabilities surround the parent-child relationship. Parents may hesitate to share their own fears, fearing the burden it may place on the child, while children may avoid expressing their vulnerabilities, fearing judgment or rejection.

3. Misunderstood Intentions:

Communication is not only about the words spoken but also about the intentions behind them. Often, parents and children fail to grasp each other's intentions accurately, leading to misinterpretations and unspoken conflicts. These misunderstandings can create a void that widens over time, leaving crucial sentiments unexpressed.

4. Unresolved Resentments:

Like any relationship, parent-child dynamics are not immune to conflicts. Arguments, disagreements, and unaddressed issues can fester beneath the surface, leading to unspoken resentments. The fear of confrontation and the desire to maintain harmony prevent both parents and children from expressing their true emotions, leaving unresolved tensions lingering between them.

5. Unacknowledged Gratitude and Affection:

While love and gratitude often exist between parents and children, they are not always openly expressed and appreciated. The assumed understanding of affection can be detrimental, as unspoken gratitude can leave parents feeling unappreciated, and unexpressed affection can leave children yearning for validation. This unspoken affection, if left unattended, can gradually erode the foundation of the relationship.

The realm of unspoken words between a parent and child is a complex and delicate tapestry. It is a realm where expectations, fears, misunderstandings, resentments, and unacknowledged affections reside. It is crucial for both parents and children to recognize the significance of these unspoken sentiments and make conscious efforts to bridge the gap. Open and honest communication, a willingness to understand each other's perspectives, and the courage to address unresolved issues are the keys to unlocking the depths of unspoken words and fostering a stronger bond between a parent and child. Only then can the unspoken find its voice, enriching the parent-child relationship with authenticity, understanding, and love.

15

Pillars of Life: Ma and Pa - Promila Sutharsan

Promila Devi Sutharsan Huidrom is a profound and eloquent writer who enjoys writing and poetry at her best. She believes that writing a few heartfelt words can make a lot of difference. She is specialized in computer science and business studies and has worked both in India and Norway. Currently, she is a full-time writer, poet, mother, philanthropist, and social activist. She loves the science of art, the art of writing, and the words that do and make wonders. Promila has been living in Norway for about 20 years, and she is the only "Pravasi" Hindi poet from Manipur (Meitei). She writes in Hindi and English, and her future books are coming in Norwegian too. She loves the literature, philosophy, and art of this beautiful life that we all have.

Pillars of Life: Ma and Pa

Indeed, Mom and Dad are the pillars of a child or even an adult. In many cases, the reason Ma is Pillar is for her caring and loving nature and Pa is a Pillar as he is the one who gets the bread and butter in the house which is one of the most important aspects in a family. Although in today's world both Ma and Pa earn so there is a lot of role shift, role exchange and role management there. If one notices that for the Millennials it´s different but those born in 70s, 80s or even earlier, it was a usual trend that Dad usually earns, and Mom took care of the Home. There is nothing wrong in that, it's just culture changes, trend changes, values change and so on. And updating ourselves with time is good.

It's very important that at the end of the day the decision should be ours. If one marries, then the decision should be of the husband and the wife together, about the roles and responsibilities in the home.

There was a time when Dad was left out in the so-called "rat-race", now both are - nevertheless! Although a family is incomplete without dad and mom, both have their own roles and are integral part of the family. We see in today's world another trend of a "single parent". There is no harm or wrong in that, although it has its own benefits and drawbacks. There can be a long discussion about that. But traditionally a Mother´s role cannot be replaced, so is Father´s too.

If we see in the old Books, we notice the importance of Mom and Dad both, and both have their respective placements and are equally important in a society. And in all these, Dad is the one who works and earns for the living of the family.

Where Dad is in the race of work life to give a better life to the family for living and he is earning bread and butter, the attachment of the kids to the dad is lacking in such cases. There are a lot of unspoken, unsaid and unexpressed words in the heart of a baby. In some cases, it stays for a lifetime and beyond. It's hurting for the child and also for many of us to see that the child remains with that wound even when he/ she is grown up. One can easily see trends of such upbringing in a child even when he/she is grown up.

And if we see today, it's a total chaos, as both Mom and Dad are out earning for a living. The expression is not to say that the Lady cannot earn. It is noticeable that, "not earning" and "not working" is two different things. A lady can have a passive income so she is financially independent, if she is not working, that can be discussed about how can she make a passive income. A lady who quits her bright career being a very good student from a young age is something really a matter of proud as now she has raised her kids and stood for her family. "Building a child is building a Nation". And, it's the mother usually who does that. So, it cannot be called a sacrifice either! For a mother who left her bright career for her family, is in another project of building a Nation. This is also way too challenging and formidable.

Amidst all this, Motherhood is one of the best feelings a lady can have and indeed the role of a mother cannot be replaced. And, in all this, the father is left behind, when it comes to sharing of thoughts and moments with their child/children. A father usually supports the family as the Pillar – economically, but they cannot show their love and emotions as men are usually not very fluent in showing their affection. And, when the same kid grows, he/she has grudges for the father who was never there for him/her in emotional need from time to time, without having a thought from his side that he was out there to earn bread and butter for the family so that the kid(s) get their best needs, education, home. And in all this, he tries his best to give the best life he could provide to the family as the head of the house.

There needs to be a change, a revolution. Fathers need to take part in the family, as today even the lady works. And usually, it so happens that even if the lady works, the responsibility of the home boils down to the lady of the house. The thinking, the management of home and roles and responsibilities must be distributed to make the best use of time and finance. Both mother and father must come together and plan and work accordingly. A mom also needs financial independence and dad also needs to take part in the home chores and caring of the child/ children in the home.

We notice that, as human nature, a woman is more emotional and caring. And fathers have difficulty showing their emotions and they usually show it by gifting and giving financial abundance, as per their level. In this, the dad forgets that kids need appreciation and physical presence too. Kids need to play, draw, cook, and do a lot, together with their dad; such cannot be replaced by gifts and economical appreciation.

It's as simple as it can be taken. If two people come together, the man and the wife, and plan to have a baby, it's just the start. Bringing the baby to this world is not enough, the real challenge starts after the baby is born and till life remains and beyond. Both mom and dad must sit together and make decisions, if they both cannot do their roles about raising the kid or rather it's called "raising a nation". Then, it is better not bring a soul to this world who is searching for life forever, if not taken care of, by both the parents. It's important to know that bringing up a child is not an easy task, it takes an entire life of both mother and father. If they are not ready for that then better not get the child to this world and give him/her a distressed childhood.

Animals' offspring(s), start to walk right after their birth but human offspring need caring and loving till early 20´s, that is the reason we are human are not animals although we humans too come in the Animal Kingdom in the Biology as described. The Animals eat, sleep, reproduce and die. We humans too do that but there is an immense lot in between; there comes the cranial capacity. That is why we are different.

Men must change- fatherhood is not well celebrated because of the past deeds and the history and the patterns noticed in general. It's high time that men have to initiate and create history, then will the history be celebrated of fatherhood. Boviously it's been discussed in general here, and there are definitely special cases, and it may be just the reverse too, but in general this is what is discussed about parenthood at several places.

Bringing a baby to this world is easy but raising is not – it's a lifetime project. Men and women or Dad and Mom must change and do their parts.

Change now-Change forever-Change for betterment-Celebrate parenthood

-Promila Devi Sutharsan Huidrom/ Promila

March '24, Norway

16

Father's happiness..! -S. Ramasamy

———♡———

S. Ramasamy belongs to Kumbakonam, Tamil Nadu. Storytelling is his passion. Earlier, he used to write in his mother tongue, Tamil. Many of his short stories and novels have been published in Tamil magazines. But, back then, his life's struggles had put an end to his storytelling. After a break of around fifteen years, he now again resumes storytelling.

♡♡♡

Father's happiness..!

Kavin had slept, as usual, with his mouth partly open. Iniya, his elder sister, gently shook his shoulder and whispered, "Kavin." He opened his drowsy eyes and saw Iniya sitting beside him on the bed. Irritated, he asked, "What?" She whispered, "I have to talk to you." Hearing the soft tenor in her voice, he understood she was after a favor. He vigorously shook his head and said, "No... I'm sleepy. This morning you slapped my back, and it pained me till I went to school," and he turned his head to sleep again.

"Ah... sorry, my little bro. I will never slap you again," she said, caressing his back. "It's about Dad's birthday." Kavin turned his head to her with shining eyes, but they instantly went dull. "But Dad never permitted us to celebrate his birthday." She nodded, "Yes, but this is his 50th birthday, so a surprise celebration would be awesome!" Seeing his hopeless look, she took his arm and said, "Dad has given us a lot of happy moments and celebrations. But have we ever done anything for him? Isn't it our responsibility to do that?"

He sat up hastily and nodded strongly, "Sure, we must. Let's call our friends too and order a big cake... pineapple flavored."

That was his favorite flavor, not hers, but she had to agree.

In the morning, they both sneaked into the kitchen when their father had gone to take a bath. The kitchen air was filled with the aroma of ghee-fried cashews. Mother was stirring a bowl on the stove, making 'Sweet Kesari,' her usual way of celebrating her husband's birthday. When they explained their plan to Mother, she squinted at them doubtfully. After hundreds of 'please, Mom' and endearments, she agreed.

While Kavin adjusted his school bag and got on his bicycle, he saw Iniya stepping out and walking towards her. He called her, "Akka, on the way to your college, can you please order the cake, pineapple flavored?" She pouted and slapped him on the back, "Don't say it aloud! Dad is inside."

Kavin frowned at her. "Hey, last night you told me you would never slap me again."

She raised her eyebrows. "Oh, you mean this is a slap? I just patted your school bag." He wrinkled his eyebrows. "Yes, it's a slap."

She pacified him, "Ha, sorry then. Get here on time after school as we have to make arrangements. Also, invite your friends." He rode away on his bicycle without saying a word.

By evening, balloons, colorful ribbons, and glittering danglers were hanging in the hall, filling it with a festive atmosphere. They were about to leave for the cake shop when their mother came running to the door with a worried face. "Iniya, just now your dad called. He is held up at the office. They have a Minister's visit tomorrow, and he can come home only by late night."

Kavin scratched his head, and Iniya sighed. They stared at each other blankly. They had invited friends and neighbors who would start arriving in an hour. Their father, a clerk at the collector's office, often got held up at work, but they didn't expect it on this day.

After a while of silence, Iniya briskly got up and started her moped. "Kavin, get on."

He blinked. "Where?"

She shouted, "First you get on."

Half-heartedly, he sat on the pillion. He looked at her in confusion when she parked the moped at the Collector's office.

She walked quickly into the collector's waiting room. On the way, she told him they were going to meet the collector and that he had to request him to permit their dad to leave for home. She didn't even give him a chance to refuse. With rising anger toward his sister and fear about talking to a collector, he nervously followed her.

He heard Iniya's voice as if coming from a well. "Remember to mention these points: Dad's 50th birthday, and that he has never had a celebration over many years."

The peon in the waiting room recognized them and inquired. When Iniya explained, he pouted and shook his head. "I will try to pass the message to the collector's PA. If the collector agrees, I will call you."

They sat fidgeting, watching the peon. After half an hour, he called them. The magnificence of the collector's room unnerved them. They approached the collector in a stiff posture. Iniya pinched Kavin's back to prompt him. Kavin stammered and somehow delivered the two main points. But when he found himself repeating the same points and saw the collector's face wrinkling, he felt ashamed, panicked, and was about to cry.

The collector smiled and sent the peon to call their father, showing them seats before his table. Sitting on the edge, Kavin couldn't control his feelings of shame and avenged his sister by pinching her forearm below the table. When their father arrived, the collector wished him and permitted him to go home, returning around 8 PM.

And guess what... Soon Dad was home! The guests cheered on seeing them. The celebration began with a roar of cheer. They both looked at their father with pride. Dad hugged and kissed them. After the guests left, before dinner, Father called many of his friends and told them about the celebration, particularly highlighting the collector's kind gesture with delight.

Kavin and Iniya observed that the collector's gesture made their father happier than their birthday arrangements. It worried them as if their efforts went to waste with minimal importance. After Father returned to the office, Mother noticed their dull faces. When she inquired, Kavin said, "We feel Dad is happier about the collector's gesture than our arrangements."

Mom tried to console him. "Don't think like that. He was quite happy with you both; that's why he hugged and kissed you. Maybe his great office experiences make him even happier. The things that make us happy change with age and exposure, Kavin."

In bed, Kavin couldn't sleep. His mother's explanation was not enough for him. His father's loud, happy voice about the collector haunted him and wouldn't let him sleep. Even past midnight, the same thought raced through his mind.

He got up and went to Iniya and woke her. "Akka...!" Iniya, seeing Kavin with half-opened eyes, could only see his silhouette with bright eyes and teeth. He continued, "Akka, I found a way to make Dad even happier." She squinted, "What?" He nodded firmly and said, "I will become a collector." Iniya's eyes widened in surprise and she stared at him quietly.

17
The Urge to Live a Teenager's Life -Khushi Sindhi

Khushi Sindhi hails from the city of Joy, Kolkata. She reads in Class-9, Section–C of Balika Siksha Sadan. Her hobby is video editing. She loves editing videos for Instagram.

The Urge to Live a Teenager's Life

Story 1

Rohan is Isha's long-distance cousin. Isha met him after a long time. She saw him in the park while she was going to visit her best friend to discuss some problems. Rohan is a 14-year-old school student, while Isha is 12 years old.

Rohan: Hi, Isha.

Isha: Hi, Rohan.

Rohan: Where are you going now?

Isha: I'm going to meet my best friend.

Rohan: Oh... but why? What happened?

Isha: I want to tell you something about me that I can't tell my mother.

Rohan: To your mother?

Isha: Yes!

Rohan: What? You know you should tell everything to your mother first.

Isha: I know, but I can't because it's my compulsion.

Rohan: Hmm... can you tell me about the compulsion behind the secret you're hiding?

Isha: Last week, my father planned a vacation to Digha. When I returned home from school, I saw no one was there. The door was locked, and that day was embarrassing. The next day, my elder brother told me that his friends were asking him to drive our father's car. I said, "OK, let's go. I'll come with you, or I'll tell this to our father." He said, "OK."

That day we went out for 2 hours. It was amazing, and his friends were so excited. We drove 10-15 km. He also filled the car with petrol using his own money. But he asked me not to tell anyone about it.

Rohan: OMG! That's great. You shouldn't talk about it to anyone.

Isha: I know! What can I do? I'm an extrovert.

Rohan: Try to keep your mouth shut, otherwise your brother will never trust you.

Isha: OK, then I'll not talk about it to anyone.

Rohan: Yes! Bye then. It's too late.

Isha: Yeah! Bye.

Story 2

It was 4 o'clock in the evening. Raju was sitting alone in the park. He saw Nimmit and called him over. They talked about why Raju was upset. Nimmit is Raju's friend, and he has a kind nature. He is Raju's comfort zone. Both are 14 years old and school students.

Raju: Hi, Nimmit.

Nimmit: Ohh... hey, where are you going?

Raju: Never mind... what are you doing here?

Nimmit: Nothing, just waiting for my best friend.

Raju: Ohh.... Nice!

Nimmit: And, what about you?

Raju: Me.... ohh, never mind.

Nimmit: Tell me... what has happened?

Raju: OK, then. I'll tell you later.

Nimmit: Tell me right now.

Raju: OK, OK! Fine.... but first, you should make a promise.

Nimmit: Promise. But why?

Raju: It's a secret. You can't tell anyone about it.

Nimmit: OK! Fiiinnneeee!

Raju: I'm just thinking that...

Nimmit: Don't think! Let me know about it.

Raju: Sorry, sorry, OK, then.

Nimmit: Hmm... tell me now.

Raju: A few days ago, I bunked school.

Nimmit: OMG! Does your mother know about it?

Raju: Hey, wait.... I'm telling you, so don't disturb me.

Nimmit: Ohh.. sorry.

Raju: A few days ago, I bunked school, and my mother knows about it.

Nimmit: Ohh.. so why are you afraid to let anyone else know about it?

Raju: There is one more thing that my mother doesn't know.

Nimmit: What thing?

Raju: I went to a museum, but it was closed that day. So, I walked around Park Street. I got lost and couldn't remember my way home. Then, a policeman helped me. I asked him where I could find a bus, and he said, "You should know about these things!"

Nimmit: OMG! It's a bad thing you did.

Raju: I know, and that's why I didn't tell anyone about it.

Nimmit: It was an amazing adventure for you.

Raju: Yeah! I think so.

Nimmit: OK, then bye, it's getting too late.

Raju: Hmm! Bye.

I have written these stories to convey my feelings about my past experiences. I want to let you know that every student makes mistakes at a young age. Younger students often try to behave like teenagers because they think that teenage life is easier and more fun than childhood. Parents should understand what their child wants, needs, or desires to do. They often misjudge because it turns out to be different.

18
Bridges of Understanding: Tales of Love and Reconciliation
-Ms. S V Padhmalatha

❤

Ms. Padhmalatha hails from Hyderabad, India. She completed her graduation from Arts College, Anantapur. She has worked as a Director at a Pharmaceutical Company for 20 years. During the COVID period, she found her passion for reading books and writing stories, and then the story continued. Thereafter, she started a new journey as an author. For the past three years, she has been in love with writing.

❤❤❤

Bridges of Understanding: Tales of Love and Reconciliation

I will be narrating two instances of my life. One from the perspective of the child and the other from the parents.

The story I am first going to narrate encompasses the things I have noticed that happen with many children. Many such instances take a mental toll on the little kids and their brains.

As the morning sun cast its warm rays upon the sleepy town, a familiar scene unfolded in the household of Karthik. "My son, it's getting late for school," his mother called out, her voice tinged with urgency. "Please come, your bus reaches within 10 minutes."

But Karthik, nestled under his blanket, wasn't eager to face the day. "Mom, I'm not interested in going to school today," he protested weakly. "I'm not feeling well."

His mother's response was less sympathetic this time. "But yesterday, you said the same thing," she countered. "You have to go, get ready. You're always coming up with different complaints."

Desperation creeping into his voice, Karthik pleaded, "But please, Mom, today I'm really not well."

An ultimatum followed swiftly. "Karthik, get ready, or else I will beat you," his mother warned sternly.

Reluctantly, Karthik dragged himself out of bed and prepared for another day at school. The journey to school felt longer than usual as he battled both physical discomfort and a growing sense of dread.

Arriving at school, Karthik found himself unable to face the impending ordeal of the math class. With a heavy heart, he sought refuge in the solitude of the washroom, hoping to escape notice.

But fate had other plans. The school helper stumbled upon him and, with a mix of concern and suspicion, reported his presence to the principal.

Summoned to the principal's room, Karthik struggled to articulate his distress. "I'm not well," he insisted, weaving a tale of imaginary ailments. "I had motions, so I was in the washroom."

Despite his efforts to evade scrutiny, Karthik found himself back in the classroom, feeling like a prisoner awaiting judgment. His friend Pruthvi, ever perceptive, sensed his distress and offered a sympathetic ear.

"What happened? Are you all right?" Pruthvi inquired, his brow furrowed with concern.

Karthik, his voice barely above a whisper, confessed his struggles with math and the fear of his mother's wrath. "I don't like it," he confessed. "It all looks like a doll to me."

Encouraged by Pruthvi's understanding, Karthik shared his apprehensions about tuition, where the tutor's discipline bordered on cruelty.

As the bell rang and the math teacher assumed command, Karthik's anxiety reached a crescendo. When confronted about his homework, he stood silent, his silence a shield against the impending storm.

But the teacher's patience wore thin, and with a swift stroke of his stick, he meted out punishment. Karthik winced as pain blossomed in his hands, the physical agony a cruel echo of his inner turmoil.

In the days that followed, Karthik's struggle with math only intensified. His mother, unaware of his silent suffering, continued to harbor lofty expectations, oblivious to the toll it exacted on her son's spirit.

As the curtain fell on another chapter of Karthik's tumultuous journey, the lingering question remained - how could a mother's concern and a child's anguish exist in such stark contrast, separated by a chasm of misunderstanding and unspoken pain?

Here, it seems children like Karthik may want to convey several messages to their parents:

1. Understanding: Children want their parents to understand their struggles and difficulties, whether it's related to health issues, academic challenges, or emotional stress.

2. Support: Rather than resorting to threats or forceful measures, children need support from their parents. This support could involve listening to their concerns, providing encouragement, and seeking appropriate help when needed.

3. Communication: Children may find it hard to express their feelings openly, especially if they fear punishment or dismissal. Parents should encourage open communication and create a safe space for their children to share their thoughts and concerns without judgment.

4. Recognition of Individual Needs: Every child is different, with unique strengths and weaknesses. Parents should acknowledge and respect their child's individual needs, whether it's in academics, extracurricular activities, or personal preferences.

5. Avoiding Pressure: Pressuring children to excel in a particular subject or activity can lead to stress and anxiety. Parents should encourage their children to do their best while also understanding that it's okay to have areas where they may struggle.

6. Advocacy: Parents should advocate for their children's well-being, whether it's addressing issues with teachers or seeking additional support, such as tutoring or counseling, if needed.

Overall, children want their parents to be understanding, supportive, and responsive to their needs, fostering an environment where they feel valued and empowered to navigate challenges with confidence.

But there are instances when parents might expect their children only to come back to them and nothing much. My neighbor faced something like this. She died in the wait of her daughter Geetha. She kept on requesting Geetha's brother Rohan to bring his sister to meet her but by the time she arrived, it was too late.

One day, Rohan noticed his father's somber mood as he prepared for work. With empathy, he reassured his father that he would mend the strained relationship by arranging a meeting with his sister, Geetha. Geetha had left her house several years back in order to marry the love of her life.

Prompted by Rohan's initiative, Geetha and her daughter arrived at their father's house, surprising him with their unexpected visit. Overwhelmed with emotion, their father welcomed them warmly, expressing his gratitude for their presence. As they settled into conversation, Rohan, caught up with work, was called upon to check on his family's reunion, reaffirming his commitment to their reconciliation.

Geetha, initially apprehensive, gradually opened up to her father, prompted by her daughter's comforting presence. Through heartfelt dialogue, they addressed past grievances and misunderstandings, finding solace in forgiveness and understanding. Their father, reflecting on the passage of time, emphasized the importance of cherishing familial bonds and letting go of past resentments.

Touched by her father's words and reminiscences of their mother's love, Geetha acknowledged her mistakes and sought forgiveness, pledging to mend their fractured relationship. With tears of remorse and gratitude, she embraced her father's reassurance and vowed to rebuildtheir bond.

Geetha, overwhelmed with emotion, expressed her remorse for neglecting her family in pursuit of her own happiness, seeking forgiveness and reconciliation.

In a poignant moment, Geetha fell at her father's feet, acknowledging her faults and pledging to honor her mother's memory by embracing her family wholeheartedly. Through their shared tears and forgiveness, they found closure and a renewed commitment to cherish each other, united by love and understanding.

The moral of the above story revolves around the importance of familial love, forgiveness, and reconciliation. It highlights the following key lessons:

1. Cherishing Family Bonds: The story emphasizes the significance of valuing and nurturing relationships within the family. Despite past misunderstandings and disagreements, the characters ultimately prioritize their family ties, recognizing them as sources of strength and support.

2. Forgiveness and Understanding: Through forgiveness and understanding, the characters are able to heal past wounds and reconcile their differences. They demonstrate the importance of letting go of grudges and resentments in order to move forward and rebuild relationships.

3. Communication and Reconciliation: Effective communication and openness facilitate reconciliation and healing. By expressing their feelings and acknowledging their mistakes, the characters pave the way for reconciliation and renewed closeness.

Overall, the moral underscores the enduring power of love, forgiveness, and reconciliation in overcoming past grievances and strengthening familial bonds.

19
The silence of addiction
-Tejaswi Kalra

Tejaswi Kalra is a postgraduate from IIT, Kharagpur. He currently oversees the family business in Varanasi. An avid reader himself, Tejaswi took to writing during college. His works have appeared in various anthologies, apart from a few solo ventures, which include a poetry book titled *Sparrow on the Bark* published under his pen name 'Tanay'. His writing carries an emotional depth as he observes the world from his unique perspective and tries to pen it down.

The silence of addiction
My hands move to a rhythm,
spending hours making the right measure,
the eyes tired and blurry vision,
mind surrendering to the pleasure,
it's the passion for liquor,
doesn't fade away for the weekend,
drowning in the taste bitter,
bringing in Mondays often saddened,

cause there will be no barley or wheat,
preserved for ages,
to manage the headache's presence sweet,
but I am diabetic,
I'd like to force my mind to freedom,
and drink till the throat goes sore,
or someone in the room passes out,
and the group keeps it discreet.
So much so that father doesn't
seem to talk about it at all,
he may have a hint,
that's speculation from my end,
can't pin point at what he's thinking,
but I get a feeling he'd be disappointed,
more than the poor grades,
the sedation on a regular,
may cost us the bond,
living may turn sour,
much like the taste of whiskey,
I rinse my mouth with
when brushing my teeth,
it's an unsaid addiction,
and for him, understated grief.
Things have gotten out of hand,
if you overhear him talking to one of his friends,
after mother's demise,
it's been a regular affair,
for him to drink his tea alone,
and me sipping on whiskey's chime,
I never had a liking for tea,
probably he had for sour mash,
but time changed the course of tongue,
which now relishes the tea leaves,

of the first flush,
maybe I'll live long enough to
have the same for myself,
till then I am a bee for him,
light head buzzing for a chunk,
amidst all the worry on the side kept.

20

Lessons Learned, Lessons Passed -Darshana Hegde

Darshana is an amateur writer, navigating the vast expanse of the world of writing. With a background in number crunching, a Chartered Accountant hailing from Mumbai, and over 16 years of corporate experience, she finally found herself in the serene landscapes of Ontario, Canada. After discovering her passion for language, she found solace and expression in the art of words, dabbling in poetry, and curating tales from her own life.

Darshana is a spoken English coach, enabling her learners to engage in fluent conversations in all spheres of life. Indulging in local food and knowing about different cultures and ways of life is what inspires her to travel. She is very fond of street photography, and also loves to capture special moments during her trips to foreign lands.

So, whether you're here for poetry or prose, or just to hang out, she'll strive to make it worth your while.

ᖚᖚᖚ

Lessons Learned, Lessons Passed

Honestly, I have a preference for the arrivals section of airports over departure terminals. Any guesses why? Goodbyes. Goodbyes tug at my heartstrings. Sometimes they hurt so much that it becomes the most enduring part of the journey. Even worse, unsaid goodbyes.

Unsaid goodbyes are a difficult proposition to come to terms with, especially when you lose your close one. A parent, for instance. I lost my father a few years ago and it was one of the most painful moments of my life. It was sudden, it was unexpected. But I'm not here to grieve.

Rather, I want to make a point about all the unsaid things that have a way of lingering in the back of our minds. The weight of unfinished conversations or unexpressed feelings can be burdensome.

I read an interesting line somewhere - the bond between parent and child is like Wi-Fi, sometimes it's strong and other times it's totally disconnected. How true? As parents we want the best for our children, and as children, we have our opinions, our beliefs and sometimes, the need for freedom. The need to be unchained and free. Free of expectations!

Often, we find ourselves struggling to find the right words or the right moment to talk and share our true feelings. I'm unsure if this situation is more prevalent now, because we have started overthinking. I find asking myself "Am I saying the right thing? Is my tone condescending? Am I being disrespectful?"

Throwback to my growing up years - my father was always a pillar of strength and wisdom in my life. Baba, as we called him, was not one to preach or lecture; instead, he taught us important life lessons through his actions. A simpleton at heart, his warm and cheerful smile was contagious. He believed in leading by example, and he did so with a quiet grace that left a lasting impact on all of us. He believed in celebrating tiny moments and small victories.

To my father, integrity, empathy, and humility were not just words but guiding principles that shaped his character. A self-made man, I admired him for staying true to his beliefs even when faced with challenges or adversities. But I never told him that….Looking back, I just wish I had expressed how much he meant to me. I loved him, and he knew that, but I wonder why I didn't say it out loud more often. It's akin to an intricate choreography of what might have been, what ought to have been, and what lingers unspoken.

We often struggle to say some things out loud that matter the most. Sometimes, expressing love is also difficult, isn't it? Is it so hard to say what we feel?

As I reflect on the invaluable lessons my father imparted to me, I am reminded of the overwhelming responsibility to pass down this treasure to my son. It is not easy, ensuring that his legacy of values lives on, but I aim to do that by sharing his stories.

The object of my affection – dad's scooter, which was famous for many reasons. My school was within walking distance from our apartment, in one of the suburbs of Mumbai (then called Bombay). My favourite memories are when baba would drop me off at school on his scooter. I would hop on with delight and proudly ride pillion on that brief five-minutes ride to school, waving out to my school mates who walked to school. Then there were times when I forgot my homework at home or the right coloured hair ribbons - every Wednesday we had to wear black instead of white. He would go back and fetch those for me.

On rainy days, I wore a raincoat and sat on the scooter, holding out an umbrella for him, but I remember him getting drenched, and not complain. Yes, that was the catch. He never complained! He gracefully accepted whatever life gave him, joys and sorrows alike.

One day while going to school, I had kept a brand-new yellow raincoat on the extra space behind, on the scooter, but alas! It fell off on the way and I realised it only after reaching school. Baba went back looking for it, but someone else got lucky. It was a different type of raincoat with a new style of pockets and slits in the front for arms, but it wasn't for me. I remember being sad and scared too, fearing a good scolding, but baba didn't shout at me.

Then there were days when the scooter would refuse to start and the engine did not budge during winter mornings. As the years went by, whenever we started our scooter in the morning, it would make this really loud screeching noise. It was so loud that everyone in the neighbourhood knew we were off to school. I remember being embarrassed then, but today I can trade anything to relive those moments.

My teachers and schoolmates knew us as the father-daughter-duo-who-rode-to-school. These memories bring smiles, goosebumps and even makes me teary-eyed, and I feel thoroughly blessed to have had such a doting father. My younger sister was enrolled in another school, and I'm sure she has her share of beautiful memories.

When I look back, I wish I would have hugged him a little more often, thanked him more for all the good things he did for seven decades of his well-lived life. I wish he would have got to spend a few years more with his grandson, and my son would also have memories for life. He was barely three when he lost his granddad, but I am grateful and glad for those precious moments.

This also further cemented the relationship with my mother. Despite having differences of opinion over some things, that doesn't make us love each other less.

Let's face it, no relationship is perfect. Even with your closest family members, disagreements are an everyday part of life. In the case of me and my mom, we definitely have our fair share of differences in opinion. From the proper way to cook a particular recipe to doing the laundry, we don't always see eye to eye.

But here's the thing – despite these differences, our love for each other always emerges a winner. I may run out of patience, but I've learned to navigate our disagreements with understanding and a healthy dose of humour. Because let's be real, sometimes you just have to laugh at the absurdity of arguing over the best way to fold laundry. In the grand scheme of things, we must learn to ignore petty squabbles and appreciate what truly matters.

A quote close to my heart goes like - The best thing to hold onto in life is each other.

There are always a bunch of things that remain unsaid. Most of us have felt unsaid but heartfelt gratitude and love at some point in our lives, only to think about it later. May we have no regrets, no sorrows over unexpressed love. Tell your children how much you love them and that you wish the best for them. Tell your parents how much blessed you are for being a part of their lives. You never know, it could be the last spoken word, the last hug.

Afterword

As I bring this book to a close, I find myself reflecting on the delicate threads that bind parents and children—threads woven from love, hope, expectations, and sometimes, misunderstandings. *The Unsaid Between a Parent and a Child* is more than just a collection of thoughts; it is a journey into the hearts of those who love deeply but often struggle to find the right words to express that love.

In writing this book, I sought to give voice to the unspoken emotions that linger in the spaces between us. The unsaid words, the silent glances, and the unexpressed fears that shape our relationships. These are the moments that define the bond between a parent and a child, yet they are often the hardest to articulate.

Every story, every experience shared within these pages, is a testament to the universal truth that while words are powerful, silence can sometimes speak even louder.

As you close this book, I hope you carry with you a renewed sense of understanding and compassion for the complex and often unspoken dynamics that exist within your own relationships. Let this be a reminder that while not every feeling needs to be voiced, acknowledging and respecting the emotions of both parent and child can pave the way for a more meaningful and fulfilling connection.

Thank you for allowing me to share this journey with you. May the stories within these pages inspire you to listen more intently, love more deeply, and cherish the beautiful, intricate bond that exists between parent and child.

- Ananya Anurag Anand

9 798889 556564 3